JOURNEY THROUGH

THE ANCIENT AND SACRED SITES

OF

GREECE

Arsinée Donoyan

Conception, design, editing and photography: Arsinée Donoyan

Printed by CreateSpace, an Amazon.com Company

Legal Deposit, 2017, Bibliothèque Nationale du Québec and National Library of Canada

Library and Archives Canada Cataloguing in Publication

ISBN-13: 978-0-9959227-0-9

Copies of this book may be ordered through:
http://www.arsineedonoyan.com

Table of Contents

Acknowledgments

To my children Tania and Armen, and my dear friends, for their encouragement and support.

Disclaimer

The information provided within this book is for general information and entertainment purposes only. Every effort has been made to make this book as accurate as possible. However, there may be typographical and/or content errors. Therefore, this book should serve only as a general guide and not as the ultimate source of subject information. All distances mentioned are approximate. The author shall have no liability or responsibility to any person or entity regarding any loss or damage incurred, or alleged to have incurred, directly or indirectly, by the information contained in this book.

Preface

Whenever the name Greece is mentioned, the image of beautiful islands with their trademark of blue sea and white houses pop up in our head. However, with *Journey Through the Ancient and Sacred Sites of Greece*, I will take you on a trip through the landscapes and mountains of the Peloponnese, covered with olive orchards and pine forests, along the seashores of the Aegean Sea, the Ionian Sea and the Corinthian Gulf, to discover the ancient and sacred archeological sites perched on hills and mountains, overlooking the sea; and then to heart-stopping and mesmerizing Meteora, driving through cotton fields, before returning to Athens.

Through my camera lens, you will discover the ancient sites such as Epidaurus, Mycenae, Nafplio, Mystras, Olympia, Delphi, marvel at heavenly Meteora, walk through the streets of Nafplio, Sparta, Athens, and drive through the little villages nestled in between. The short descriptions accompanying the photos give only a general idea of these magnificent sites charged with so much history, beauty and power.

An eight-day organized bus tour where I am in constant awe at every turn of the road or cliff. An intense history and outstanding geography course highlighted with Greek hospitality, healthy Mediterranean food and, above all, a dream come true!

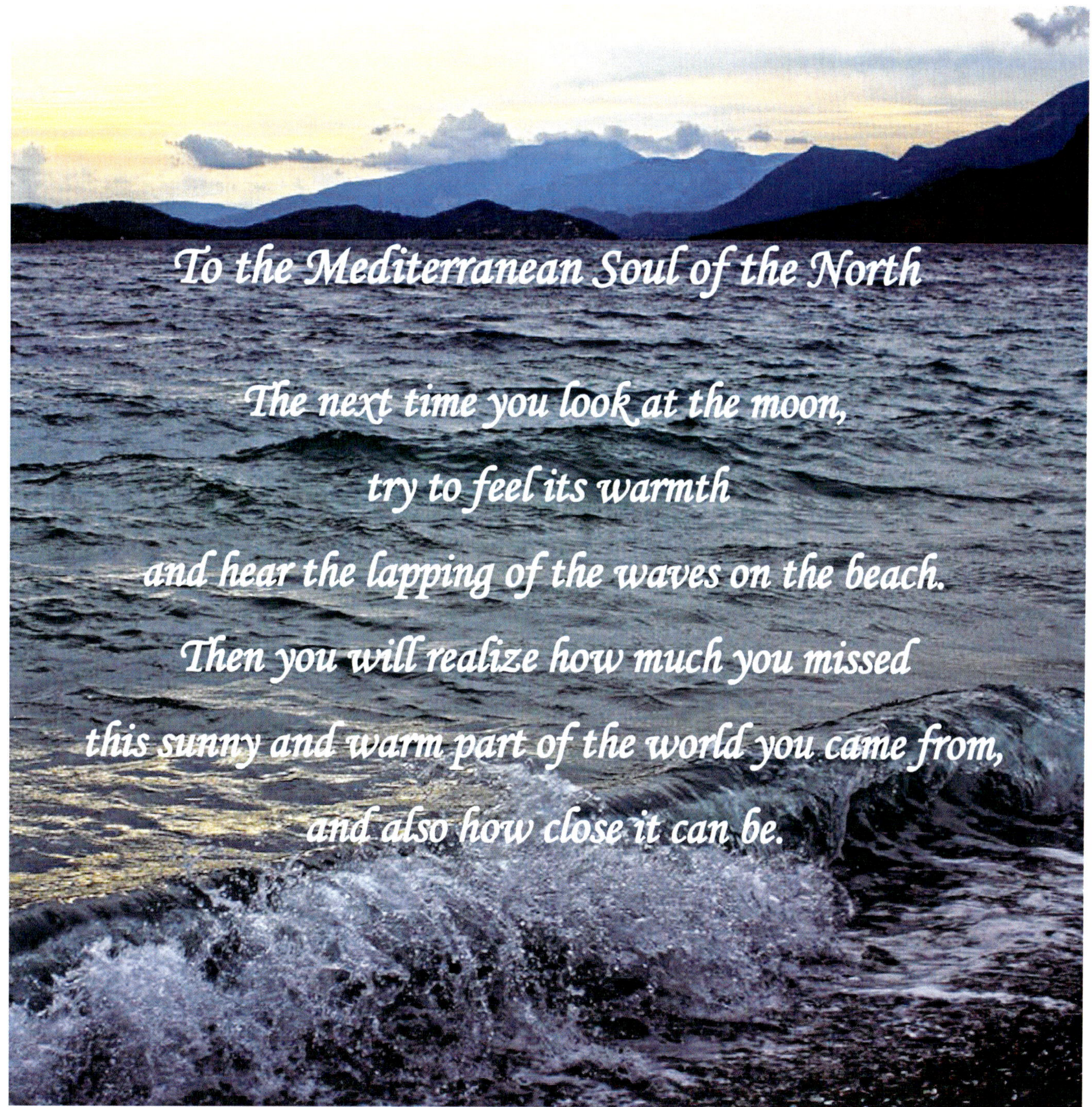
To the Mediterranean Soul of the North
The next time you look at the moon,
try to feel its warmth
and hear the lapping of the waves on the beach.
Then you will realize how much you missed
this sunny and warm part of the world you came from,
and also how close it can be.

Meteora
Kalabaka Μετέωρα
Καλαμπάκα
Larissa
Λάρισα
Trikala
Τρίκαλα
Palamas
Παλαμάς
Karditsa
Καρδίτσα
Farsala
Φάρσαλα
Volos
Βόλος
Almiros
Αλμυρός
Skiathos
Σκίαθος
Skopelos
Σκόπελος
Arta
Άρτα
Karpenissi
Καρπενήσι
Lamia
Λαμία
Thermopylae
Θερμοπύλαι
Agrinio
Αγρίνιο
Amfissa
Άμφισσα
Delphi
Δελφοί
Arachova
Αράχοβα
Parnassus
Itea
Ιτέα
Livadia
Λειβαδιά
Nafpaktos
Ναύπακτος
Clovino Beach
Missolonghi
Mesolongi
Patras
Πάτρα
Aigio
Αίγιο
Thiva
Θήβα
Kalavrita
Καλάβρυτα
Mount Kyllini
Corinth
Κόρινθος
Athens
Αθήνα
Rafina
Ραφήνα
Mati
Μάτι
Salamina
Egina
Peloponnese
Amaliada
Αμαλιάδα
Pyrgos
Πύργος
Archea
Olimpia
Αρχαία
Ολυμπία
Kaiafas
Καϊάφας
Zacharo
Ζαχάρω
Mycenes
Μυκῆναι
Argos
Άργος
Nafplion
Ναύπλιο
Tolo
Tripoli
Τρίπολη
Epidavros
Επίδαυρος
Poros
Πόρος
Spetses
Σπέτσες
Kalamata
Mystras
Sparti
Σπάρτη
Map data ©2017 Google
Google

Day 1

Mati - Μάτι

The flight from France is at 11:15 a.m. and we arrive in Athens at 2:30 p.m. (Athens time is one hour ahead). As soon as we pick up our luggage at the airport, we are greeted by the travel agency representatives and there we go off to the hotel in Mati on the outskirts of Athens by the Aegean Sea.

I make sure I sit in front of the taxi. I want to take in as much as I can. Finally! After so many years, here I am on Greek soil. It is a beautiful, warm and sunny day. The mountains along the road lead the way. I haven't seen anything yet and I already find the country so beautiful. I strike a conversation with the driver. To my question as to where the city center is situated, he shows me the mountains and tells me it's behind them. No luck to have a peak of Athens this afternoon.

After a 45 minute drive, we arrive at the hotel. It's right on the beach! Nothing fancy but a nice view on the Aegean Sea. It is already 6:00 p.m. A bit cool to go for a swim; although, it does not seem to deter some enthusiasts to go for a dip along the shore. I take off my shoes, roll up my jeans. I want to walk on the sand and feel the waves. Alas, as soon as I walk down the ramp to the beach, I realize it is covered with big rocks and pebbles. I settle for a lawn chair by the poolside, feeling the late afternoon sun, breathing the ocean air and gazing at the horizon, admiring the sea and the hills afar … I am in Greece!

Mati is a small popular holiday town with a marina situated 40 km (25 miles) east of Athens, on the Aegean Sea.

Dinner is in the form of a buffet. Simple but tasty and fresh. No doubt one has to come to Greece to taste the best *Moussaka* (eggplant dish). After dinner, I walk down the street, avid to discover the area. My adventure does not take me far. Except for few typical Greek *tavernas*, there is not much to discover. The taverns, hidden behind climbing bushes of bougainvillea in flower are inviting with their dim lights, but it is getting late and time to get back to the hotel. Tomorrow morning, we hit the road at 8:30 a.m.

In the middle of the night, I am awakened by the annoying buzz of a mosquito. In the dark, I try to hit it hoping to kill the damn intruder. Little I know that I will barely sleep that first night. No "*kali nihta*" (good night)! How silly of me to leave the balcony door open so I could sleep with the sound of the waves lapping on the shore ... Obviously, drawing the drapes in front of the balcony door so not to let any insect inside the room did not work. What was I thinking? An army of mosquitos have a feast that night and I, for the next few days, have my arms and hands tattooed with their sweet bites. No, they are not sweet *zouzounakis (endearing term meaning little bugs)*; it is a vicious extraterrestrial blood thirsty swarm of welcoming mosquitos!

During our entire trip, every morning, we have breakfast and dinner at wherever hotel we stay, both in the form of a buffet. Not gourmet but fresh and plenty. For breakfast, I have a glass of orange juice, biscotti with Greek yogurt and jam, and a cup of coffee without forgetting those grape-must cookies spiced with lots of cinnamon.

Every morning, we leave the hotel with our luggage as the bus continues the circuit and we never know ahead of time where we will sleep that night. It is tiresome to drag our luggage every morning but at the same time exciting to look forward to try a new place. Each hotel and each restaurant where we dine for lunch is nicely chosen. In all these restaurants/taverns, we are served and each day the menu varies, but they all have these hot red tomatoes in their salads. When I say red, I mean RED down to the core, and delicious! Grapes being in season, large portions of grapes are served almost at every lunch.

Along the road, the bus makes few stops to let us stretch our legs, use the washrooms and purchase few items to take back home. The trick is not knowing if at the next stop, they will have the same items or a better choice. A guessing game which also means to forget the plan of buying the souvenirs the last day of the trip so not to overload the suitcase from day one. As the days go by, my suitcase is getting heavier and heavier. Of course, we have *Loukoumi* (sweets), pistachios, honey and even Greek wine back at home, but it feels more fulfilling to buy them right in Greece, and you bet they taste better!

We are a group of 47 tourists, all from different parts of France. We have the nicest and the best bus driver ever. To drive through the narrow mountainous roads, I feel less nervous with a competent driver. As for our guide, she knows French perfectly and she is very knowledgeable. Unfortunately, being a large group and our guide giving so much detail in a low tone voice, I often prefer to concentrate on taking photos rather than listening to her explanations. A tough choice but I rely on books and other sources of information to find what I am missing in her explanations.

I am thrilled to get to sit right behind the driver. Yess! I could take photos even when the bus is rolling. Surprisingly, quite a number of the photos taken from the bus on the move are of good quality.

I am impressed by the road conditions and how well the roadsides are landscaped. All along, there are these firethorn/pyracantha bushes with small clusters of orange color wild berries that brighten the landscape.

The most moving part of my entire trip is to walk on the land where thousands of years ago various civilizations came and went, entire populations lived, carried rituals, built amazing structures without any of the technologies that we possess today. They were evolved human beings who believed in mythology, in deities, but nevertheless, they were human beings who had the same basic needs as us. Little they knew that centuries later, their ruins will be visited by millions of people from all over the world.

This is more than a trip or a vacation. This is a long time due pilgrimage. Camera on hand, I want to capture every scenery, every stone, every tree. In spite of being surrounded by a large number of tourists, I often feel as though I am alone. Alone with my thoughts, lost in the past.

Day 2

Corinth Canal - Διώρυγα της Κορίνθου

First day of our trip! A sunny and bright morning! We drive a little over an hour from Mati before arriving at the Corinth Canal. Take few photos of the Canal, buy some *loukoumi*, pistachios. After having given up the initial plan to stay few days on the Island of Aegina, the pistachio heaven, this is as close as I am going to get to a fresh bag of pistachios. Of course, a bag of Corinth raisins is in order as well. You cannot come all the way to Corinth and not taste the fruit right on the land where it originated in 75 BCE.

The Corinth Canal connects the Ionian Sea and the Saronic Gulf in the Aegean Sea through the Gulf of Corinth. It is 6.3 km (3.9 miles) long and 21.4 meters (70 feet) wide with its sides rising as much as 90 meters (295 feet). The initial digging was inaugurated in 67 CE by Nero but abandoned, and finally completed in 1893.

Mycenae - Μυκήνες

Our next stop takes us to Mycenae, the oldest city on the mainland of Greece, situated in the northeast side of the Peloponnese, at 120 km (74.5 miles) southwest of Athens. The citadel of Mycenae is built on a hill with a great view in the middle of mountains and olive orchards. What a gorgeous landscape! We walk through Lion's Gate; visit the ruins of the Citadel, the Treasury of Atreus (Agamemnon's tomb). I try to imagine how this place looked like when it was inhabited, and I can't believe I am here walking on the same grounds. It is a pleasantly hot and sunny day, and I am trying to register in my memory every single detail.

The archeological site Mycenae is located on the hills of Panagitsa in the plain of Argolis. The Mycenaean civilization dominated from 1600 BCE to 1200 BCE. They were the first people to speak an ancient form of the Modern Greek language. It is still debated what caused the end of the Mycenaeans (earthquake, invasion, in-fighting) which was followed by the Greek Dark Ages.

The Treasury of Atreus, a beehive shaped tholos tomb, was built between 1350 and 1250 BCE named after King Atreus. It is also known as the Tomb of Agamemnon (Atreus'son), the legendary king of Mycenae, although some scholars believe his actual tomb is outside the walls of the city.

The Treasury of Atreus / Tomb of Agamemnon

Dome inside the Treasury of Atreus

The Lion Gate marks the entrance to the citadel of Mycenae.

The Grave Circle A was discovered by the German archeologist Heinrich Schliemann in 1876. It is believed to have served as a burial site to Agamemnon's predecessors of three centuries, and not Agamemnon. The famous "Death Mask of Agamemnon" was discovered by Schliemann in Mycenae.

The Grave Circle A

Lunch is at an open air tavern/restaurant in Mycenae where we are treated to Greek hospitality by having a pile of dishes smashed on the floor to welcome us, causing quite a startle before realizing it is not one of the waiters who slipped with his tray of food. Roasted lamb, fries, salad. Everything tastes so fresh and delicious. I engage in a conversation with a couple from our group who decides to share our table. Neither of us have any clue that this couple from Paris and I, we have a very dear common friend back in Paris! I still can't get over it. Of course, our common friend in Paris is surprised more than ever to receive a photo of both her best friends vacationing together in Greece! *Que le monde est petit!* Talk about a small world!

Nafplio is where we are heading next, an approximate of a thirty minute drive.

Nafplio - Ναύπλιο

Nafplio is the perfect charming town: history, scenic view, lovely streets, colorful houses, very quaint and romantic. The ideal place for lovers to stroll through the tiny streets, sip a glass of wine at a terrace and gaze into each other's eyes … On the main boulevard, along the shore, palm trees spread their shade over the passersby and outdoor restaurants while pleasure boats line the seashore across.

As soon as we are set free to visit the town on our own for one hour, I take off with my camera to discover this little gem. The taverns on the back narrow streets are quiet. The bougainvilleas are everywhere, showing off their beautiful colorful flowers on the balconies, on the walls, at the building entrances. It must be nap time for the locals as I am the only one walking on the streets on this beautiful sunny September afternoon. Time has stopped. A dog from a nearby tavern runs towards me. Very friendly. I want to take its photo but it is already back in the tavern. I start walking faster as I have very little time left before joining the group. I wish I could just sit at one of the tables, have a *café frappé* (iced coffee) and enjoy the beautiful afternoon!

I arrive at the town square taking photos right and left. No time to pause and assess. At large, in the Argolic Gulf, there stands the Castle of Bourtzi. Few clicks to immortalize the Castle, and a last shot of the ruins of the Fortress of Palamidi perched on the hills over the town, and we are already back on the road.

Handwoven
Textiles

Dimello

ΛΙΜΕΝΕΡΓΑΤΩΝ

St. Nicholas Church built in 1713 and restored in 1836.

Philellinon Square – Monument built in 1903 in memory of the French philhellenes who fought and died for the liberation of Greece from the Turks.

Nafplio, a seaport town on the Argolic Gulf was the capital of the First Hellenic Republic from 1821 until the capital was moved to Athens in 1834. Throughout centuries, the Byzantines, Franks, Venetians and Turks have left their mark on its architecture.

Built in 1473 in the middle of the harbour of Nafplio, in the Argolic Gulf, the Castle of Bourtzi served as a fortress until 1865. It has also been used as the residence of the executioner of the Fortress of Palamidi, and converted to a hotel from 1930 to 1970. It now hosts music festivals in summer while remaining a major tourist attraction.

The Fortress of Palamidi was built by the Venetians between 1711 and 1714. For a period of time, it was also used as a prison. It can be reached by the road or the steps. There are close to 1000 steps from the town to the fortress.

Epidaurus - Επίδαυρος

Epidaurus is our next destination. A drive of 36 km (22 miles). I have read so much about the tall pine trees in the park at Epidaurus that I cannot wait to step foot on the site. Few cafés on each side of the large walk leading to the site offer freshly squeezed orange juice to quench our thirst. To reach the amphitheater, we have to walk uphill through a path lined with pine trees. It is now 4 o'clock in the afternoon, the sun is not as strong and I am starting to feel tired. One last effort and I am at the ancient amphitheater. There is barely anyone else except for our group. Not enough time to neither walk up above the amphitheater, nor visit the Sanctuary of Asklepios as the site will soon close for the day and we still have to visit the museum. I share the bench with a kitten who seems fast sleep; take a deep breath of the air filled with pine tree fragrance. It is overwhelming to experience such a serene surrounding with air so pure and nature so beautiful.

Located on the northeastern side of the Peloponnese, in the region of Argolis, the ancient theater in Epidaurus was built in late 4th Century BCE. It seats 13,000 spectators and it is renowned for its architecture and acoustics where the actors in the center can be perfectly seen and heard by all spectators. It is still used today for performances during festivals.

In the 2nd Millennium BCE, the Sanctuary of Asklepios was reputed for its ceremonial healings, and later as the first organized sanatorium, as well as being considered the cradle of medicine.

On the way back to the bus, I have a last look at the tall pine trees … So long, Epidaurus …

Tolo – Τολό

Once in the bus, we find out that we are spending the night in Tolo, a seaside town on the Argolic Gulf. A typical seaside vacation town where most facilities close in winter. Our hotel, not only it is on the beach, but the waters come right to the building during high tide. So happy that the room is facing the gulf with a gorgeous view of the mountains across and Koronisi Island where stands the Chapel of the Holy Apostles. Very beautiful at night when the chapel is all lit up. It is still daylight. I go downstairs looking for a way to go to the beach and walk on the sand. Me and my obsession to walk on the sand … Much to my disappointment, it is high tide and no sandy beach to walk on. That night, no lapping of the waves against the building either, I ain't leaving any patio door open. Not anticipating another mosquito raid during my sleep.

Koronisi Island. The Chapel of the Holy Apostles across the shores of Tolo.

Tolo is an old fishing village and a seasonal resort situated on the Argolic Gulf. Half an hour from Epidaurus and Mycenae, 10 minutes from Nafplio and less than 2 hours from Athens. Tolo has been successively under the Byzantine rule, the Frankish, the Venetian and the Ottoman until its liberation in 1834 by the Greeks. Throughout history, it has played an important role as a naval base. On the right, Romvi Island known also as Island of Aphrodite.

Day 3

Mystras - Μυστράς

It's a cloudy morning but by the time we finish our breakfast in the hotel restaurant by the seashore in Tolo, the sun is trying to peak through the clouds.

From Tolo to Mystras, it is a 130 km (81 miles) drive. On the way, we stop at a gift shop/factory renowned for its pottery. We have a demonstration of the process by the owner himself, buy some souvenirs and most important, an owl made of pottery to counteract evil eye, as believed in old Greek tradition.

By the time we arrive at Mystras, on the foothills of the Taygetos Mountains, there is a fine rain. So fine that you don't even feel like opening the umbrella. It is foggy and misty, adding some mysticism to the site. Such a beautiful and peaceful landscape! Again, olive trees everywhere! The fortress on top of the hill, which we cannot see because of the fog, is not accessible due to renovations and the slippery condition of the steps under the rain. The restaurant that shares the same parking as the site has the most gorgeous view of olive groves beneath, in the Eurotas Valley, and a panoramic view of Sparta.

Eurotas Valley – Misty Sparta on the horizon.

How about a cup of coffee under a laurel tree of few centuries old?

Mystras was founded in 1249 by the Franks. After their defeat by the Byzantines in 1259, Mystras flourished and became the capital of the Empire. In 1460, Mystras passed to the hands of the Ottoman Turks until its liberation by the Greeks in 1821. During the Ottoman rule, from 1687 to 1715, Mystras was ruled by the Venetians. Since, all the inhabitants have moved to the city, except for the nuns who live in the Monastery of Pantanassa.

That morning, we visit three of the Byzantine churches, St. Demetrios (Mitropolis), Odrigitria and St. Theodore (Vronthokhion). I feel as though I am on a holy pilgrimage. Here I am in St. Demetrios Church, lighting up a candle in front of a Byzantine icon, in silent prayer, while my thoughts race throughout centuries, throughout civilizations towards those who stepped foot on these same grounds, kings, princesses, clergies, merchants, the poor and the rich and the barbarians who looted and destroyed most of it turning it into a ghost town.

St. Demetrios (Mitropolis) Cathedral was built in 1270. The antechamber was added in 1291.

13th-14th Century fresco

Byzantine Icon

Roman sarcophagus

While walking through the courtyard to enter St. Demetrios Church, I notice a snail on the stairs. I am delighted. For so long, I had wanted to photograph a snail, let alone one high up on the mountains of Greece, in Mystras! Sent by heaven! My second wish is granted few minutes later when during my walk towards the next church, I come across a fig tree. With all the tourists passing by, I am not too hopeful to find any ripe figs, but a little perseverance and I am able to find few of them. Delicious! Back to the bus, and I am served to a bunch of juicy white grapes just picked from the area. Hallelujah! I am in heaven!

St. Theodore Church

St. Theodore Church built in the 13th Century in the Vronthokhion monasterial complex

Odigitria Church built in 1320-21 in the Vronthokhion monasterial complex

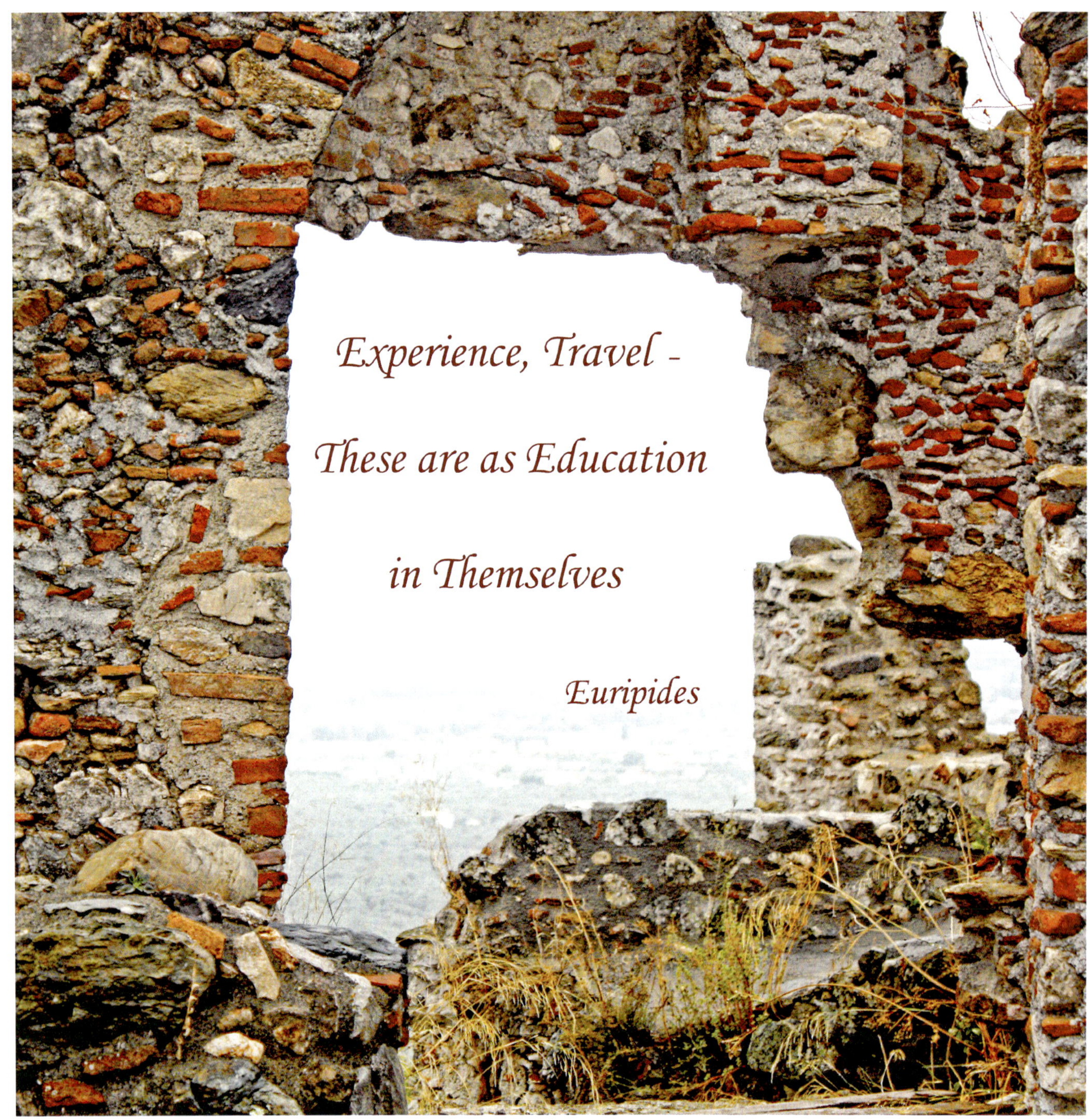
Experience, Travel -
These are as Education
in Themselves
Euripides

Sparta – Σπάρτη

While driving to Sparta for lunch, we pass on the road the Spartathlon marathon runners taking their challenge in the rain. We couldn't have picked a more memorable day to be in Sparta. So exciting to see all these runners from all over the world arrive exhausted one after the other through a cheering crowd to finally finish at the foot of Leonidas' statue in the center of the city. Another great lunch in one of the cozy restaurants, with red checkered tablecloth, on the main street. The sky is still grey but the rain has stopped.

Spartathlon, a foot race that started in 1984, takes place every year in September to trace the footsteps of Pheidippides who ran from Athens to Sparta in 490 BCE to seek help during the battle of Marathon against the Persians. The Spartathlon runners have 36 hours to run from Athens to Sparta covering 246 km (153 miles), running through hillsides, mountains, non-stop, day and night.

Kaiafas - Καϊάφας

After a two hour drive, we arrive at Kaiafas in the region of the Gulf of Kyparissia, a bay of the Ionian Sea. The hotel is situated in the middle of an olive grove. It is family run with hospitality out of this world! It is already dinner time. Our group fills up the dining room and I end up sharing the table with a couple from the Netherlands who are the only visitors not from our group. Great conversation, and the food is just amazing! Everything grown and raised on the hotel premises. Already anticipating the morning breakfast. The evening ends on a high note with the owner's teenage son and daughter playing a classical piece on the piano before performing a duo of *Sirtaki* dance where some of us in the group join in the dance. *Opa!*

At the break of dawn, I am awakened by the roosters' crows. To make the most of my travel, with eyes half closed, I step on the balcony to see the view. Through the rising sun on the right, there lies Kaiafas lake shining far on the horizon while the moon setting on the left, reveals the silhouette of Mount Lapithas covered with olive trees. An experience worth waking up early, especially to listen to the symphony of chirping crickets surpassed randomly by the roosters' cock-a-doodle-doo.

Kaiafas is located 347 km (216 miles) southwest of Athens and 20 km (12 miles) south of Olympia. It is reputed for its sulfuric thermal springs since the ancient times.

Kaiafas Lake situated between Lapithas Mountain and the Ionian Sea.

When you are awakened early in the morning by the roosters crowing, you know you are in a village, and when a hoard of goats crosses the route, that confirms it.

On the way to Olympia

Alfeios River is the longest in the Peloponnese. It takes its source in the highlands of Arcadia and empties into the Ionian Sea.

Day 4

Olympia - Ὀλυμπία

Olympia is only 11 km (6.8 miles) away from Kaiafas and the only site where we do not have to walk up a hill. It is 10:30 in the morning, the sun is shining and it is already so warm. Obviously we are not the only group up early to experience Olympia as we are surrounded by dozens of other tourist groups from all over Europe. French, English, Greek, German, Russian, all nationalities and languages intermingled so much so that one has to be alert not to follow the wrong group if they happen to share the same language as us.

The site of the ancient sanctuary of Olympia is vast. The grounds are covered with ruins of pillars; some erect towards the blue sky, others lying on the ground, some on piles, and yet others in the midst of repairs.

Temple of Hera, built around 600 BCE, where the modern day Olympic torch lighting takes place.

The Philippeion

The Crypt – the archway entrance to the Stadium.

Columns of the Temple of Zeus

Corinthian Capital

Greek inscriptions

Laurel wreath carvings

The Stadium – Site of the Ancient Olympic Games. The racetrack where the Olympic Games were held from 776 BCE to 393 CE is 212 meters (696 feet) long and 32 meters (105 feet) wide. It is said to be able to accommodate 45,000 spectators who would sit on the grass to watch the games.

Olympia is an amazingly beautiful place with pine trees everywhere. A full day is needed to visit each corner, read every inscription and to visit the museum situated half a kilometer away. Once our guide finishes her explanations at the site, we are left on our own to walk to the museum, visit it and then meet the group at the parking lot where we are told the bus will wait.

The horse drawn carriage waiting at the gate to take the tired visitors to the museum looks so appealing that I jump in thinking this is my only chance to get a carriage ride while in Greece even if it lasts ten minutes.

Before entering the museum, I decide to take some photos of the statues alongside the building. Much to my dismay, my camera refuses to click. I keep trying all the dials. Nothing. I sit on one of the benches in the courtyard to check the camera closely. Disaster! The protective lens is broken into zillion pieces. But, how did this happen? I must have banged my purse somewhere while the camera was inside. I am relieved that the actual lens is intact. I clean the camera, replace the battery, replace the memory card, hoping they are just dislodged and causing the camera not to function. Nothing!

I am now in a panic mode. No camera and we are only half way through the trip. There isn't even any possibility to purchase a new camera. The only shopping areas that the bus stops are on the highway where they sell only souvenirs and the area where we stay overnight, nothing comes close to a camera shop. I can't remember how long I sat on that bench fiddling with the camera, almost in tears, trying to find a solution. Finally after numerous attempts, I am able to take some photos but only at random on the "sport" setting. Who cares, as long as it takes some photos. As I slowly come back to reality, I look around and don't see anyone from the group. Where did everyone disappear? Before the mishap, there were some of them around. How long was I sitting on the bench? Could it be that everyone is already back to the bus?

To play it safe, I decide to find the bus in the parking lot. The guide had mentioned 'the big parking lot'. This one doesn't look big and there is no bus. At this point, I am walking back towards the Olympic site. Yes, towards the gate where I took the carriage ride. Even the astray dogs who were roaming on the grounds of the Olympic site are now crossing my path. I ask around for the 'big' parking lot, but no one seems to know where it is. The worst part is that our guide had not given us her telephone number which meant I had no way of contacting her either.

It is interesting how the mind works when in stress or in panic. I am now imagining all these scenarios where I am left behind and the group takes off without me. By now, I am walking back to the museum alongside the horse drawn carriage bringing other visitors. As I arrive back at the museum, I see the members of the group coming out of the museum one by one. I am so relieved but at the same time so disappointed as I missed the opportunity to visit the magnificent Archeological Museum of Olympia.

After a very short stop at a café, we head for lunch to a nearby tavern/restaurant, also known as an event venue. It is a feast in an amazing authentic decor and beautiful surroundings with an inviting outdoor swimming pool.

Back in the bus, I manipulate again and again the camera and try to take as many photos as possible on the 'sport' setting which I normally use it anyways when shooting from a moving vehicle. The mountains, the bay, the villages, they all become my accomplices and assist me in not giving up on the camera. We have a long haul ahead of us until Arachova where we will spend the night. We cross on a ferry the Gulf of Corinth from Rio in the North of the Peloponnese peninsula to Antirrio on the mainland of Greece.

Patras - Πάτρα / Rio-Antirrio - Ρίο-Αντίρριο

Inaugurated in 2004, the Rio-Antirrio Bridge is one of the world's longest cable-stayed bridges near Patras. It is 2,880 meters (1.8 miles) long end to end. It crosses over the Gulf of Corinth and links the Peloponnese peninsula to mainland Greece. Its design was led by the Armenian architect Berdj Mikaelian and the construction carried out by a French-Greek company.

Olympic runner in Antirrio

Corinthian Gulf

After a half an hour drive from Antirrio, we make a halt at Clovino beach in Phocis. A short walk along the shores is all the time we have to contemplate the shadows of the mountains and listen to the waves. From Antirrio until Itea, we drive along the western shores of the Corinthian Gulf. No words can describe the beautiful scenery of the mountains, the bay with its ever changing striking blue, green and turquoise waters and the villages with their brick red rooftops nestled in between.

Clovino Beach

The whole life of a man
is but a point in time.
Let us enjoy it.
Plutarch

Delphi – Δελφοί

From Itea we head northwest towards the sacred sanctuary of Delphi through the mountains. The view is so incredible, the mountains so majestic that I am filled with awe at every turn of the road. It is near dusk when we arrive in Delphi. We only have a little time to visit the Tholos and the sanctuary of Athena Pronaia as it will soon get dark. We hurry up to go down the path and suddenly, here it is, surrounded by a chain of mountains on Mount Parnassus, the ruins of the Tholos! To experience the panoramic view of the mountains, the sun setting on the right, between the mountains, the eerie silence, the air so crisp, it is understandable why this site was chosen as a sacred place. I have already fallen under its spell!

The hotel in Arachova where we spend the night is built right against the mountain rock. Popular during the ski season, it is nicely decorated with a large veranda overlooking the mountain hills. It must be astounding to see it in winter when all is covered with snow.

The sanctuary of Athena Pronaia and the Tholos, located across the road from the Temple of Apollo on Mount Parnassus. The Tholos was built in the 5th Century BCE. According to legend, Mount Parnassus was home to the Muses.

Day 5

We are on the slopes of Delphi by 9:30 a.m. It is a gorgeous morning, blue sky, warm and dry weather. By this time, I only have one thought: my camera. Every time I click, I worry that it will not work. In silence, I pray the gods. I didn't come all the way here and leave without any photos of Delphi.

On the left: the Base of the tripod of Plataea. On the right: the altar of the Chians in marble revetment. On the back: the columns of the Temple of Apollo.

It's an uphill walk and I am determined to go up as high as I can. Half way through, I take a moment to contemplate the view. I am now facing the breathtaking mountains across. Only few tourists can be seen here and there, most of them having gone ahead or returned. It is incredibly peaceful and all that can be heard is the chirping of the birds. Once again, I am overwhelmed by the pure and crisp air. I imagine the ancient Greeks going up and down the sacred path, performing various rituals, celebrations. Time has stopped. A feeling of extreme wellness reigns. I feel the positive energy. It's in the air, it's under my feet. It's magical! At that moment, I understand why I chose this trip. It is not a coincidence. This is the highlight of my pilgrimage. To reconnect with my inner self. I have come home. As I continue to climb up, I touch the rocks on the side of the path to feel its warmth. I am now well over the amphitheater but not enough time to continue all the way up to the stadium as time is pressing and I have to return to join the group. A last glance, a last panoramic photo, and then suddenly, miracle! My camera is back working normally.

Before going on this trip, I did not have the time to read in detail about the sites to be visited. I had no preconceived idea about what I was to discover, neither was there one that I preferred more than another. All I knew is that I was going to tour the Peloponnese, discover Meteora and visit the ancient archeological sites. I was not prepared to feel what I felt on the slopes of Delphi, and I thank the ancient gods of Delphi for their precious gift.

The sacred Omphalos or the navel of the Earth. According to Greek mythology, Zeus sent two eagles from opposite ends of the earth and they met at Delphi, the center of the World and it was marked by a stone. The altar of the Chians in background (left). A copy of the original Omphalos in marble at the Museum in Delphi (right).

Roman Agora – pillar

Naxian Sphinx Column

Pillar of Prussia

Rock of the Sybil

The Rock of the Sybil named after the first priestess who foretold the future. Commonly known as the Oracle of Delphi, where Pythia, a high priestess of the Temple of Apollo at Delphi served as the oracle when in trance.

The name Pythia is derived from Pytho, which in Greek mythology was the original name of Delphi, Apollo having killed there the pythia (snake) who used to guard the sacred area.

Later, the name was changed to Delphi (meaning dolphin) to mark the form Apollo took to bring safely Cretan sailors to his temple to serve as priests.

Research shows that the Temple of Apollo sat on a fault line. The ethylene from the nearby spring water would escape from the cracks in the enclosed chamber and cause the trance.

The Stoa of the Athenians, marble columns built in 478 BCE where the naval war trophies over the Persians were displayed.

In the background, the polygonal style retaining wall supporting the side of the platform of the Temple of Apollo

Stoa of the Athenians

The Sacred Way

Treasury of the Athenians – 490 BCE

The Theater – Built in the 4th Century BCE and remodeled several times. It has 35 rows and could seat 5,000. Delphi was first settled during the Mycenaeans in 1500 – 1100 BCE. In the 8th Century BCE, it became the center of worship of Apollo.

Temple of Apollo built in the 4th Century BCE – Entrance to the temple on the left side.

The popularity of Delphi declined in 385 CE and the site was gradually buried and a village built on top. In 1892, after relocating the population of the entire village, excavations began revealing the ruins.

Back to reality and off to visit the museum at the entrance before heading to the restaurant in Arachova for lunch and then off to Kalambaka (Meteora) through a rather flat land and cotton fields with a short stop at Thermopylae to visit the Memorial site of Leonidas.

Artemis

Sphinx of Naxos - 566 BCE

Apollo Cup 480-470 BCE

Dancer

Kleobis & Biton Kouroi 650-500 BCE

Dionysus

Siphnian Caryatid 525 BCE

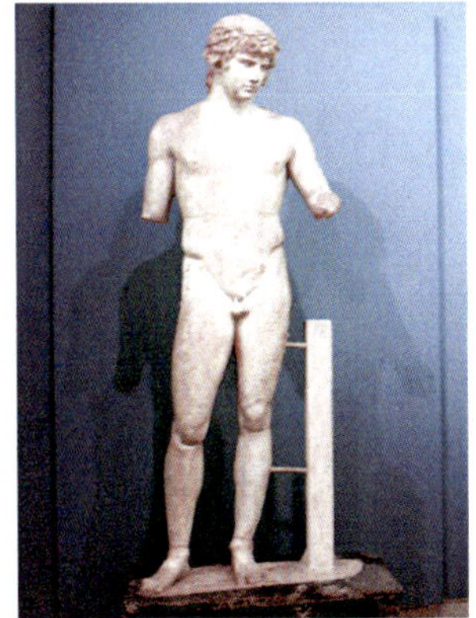

Antinous – 130-135 BCE

The Charioteer – 470 BCE

Hagias

Philosopher 280-270 BCE

Thermopylae - Θερμοπύλαι

Leonidas, king of Sparta

Eurotas (representing the river in Sparta)

Taygetos (representing the mountain in Sparta)

The Memorial site where Leonidas fell under the arrows of the Persian army in 480 BCE. Regarded as a hero, Leonidas and his 300 royal bodyguards sacrificed their life to safeguard their army and country. Later that year, the Athenian navy defeated the Persians.

It is scorching hot when we arrive for a very short visit by late afternoon in Thermopylae which means 'hot gates' named after the hot springs in the area. The memorial site is along the highway, in the middle of nowhere where the narrow battle passage was, between Mount Kalidromo and the east coast of central Greece. The fact that I am standing on the battle grounds, almost during the same month where the battle took place in August/September, gives more of a profound meaning to my experience.

As we enter the town of Kalambaka, we are greeted by the grandiose rocks of Meteora standing tall ahead of the road. It's almost 7:30 p.m. when we arrive at the hotel. Today, we covered a distance of 430 km (267 miles). The weather is a bit cool and it's starting to rain, otherwise, it would be an ideal way to wrap up the day by swimming in the hotel pool by the shadow of the imposing rocks of Meteora. We are already reaching the end of our trip. Tomorrow, we sleep in Athens …

Day 6

Meteora – Μετέωρα

Meteora which means 'suspended in the air' describes well the impression one gets when looking at these gigantic and imposing marvels. It is like being in wonderland out of a fiction movie all the while feeling so humbled.

Situated in the region of Thessaly and perched at as high as 396 meters (1,300 feet), there were initially 24 monasteries but only six remain functional: Varlaam, Roussanou, St. Nikolas Anapfsas, Holy Trinity, St. Stephens and the Great Meteoron. Since the 11th Century, hermits inhabited the caves of Meteora prior to the Greek Orthodox monks. The monasteries were built between the 14th and 16th Century to escape persecution from the Ottomans.

We arrive at Meteora by the way of the village of Kastraki. At each turn, we have a different angle of the rocks and yet another breathtaking view! We spend the entire morning driving through the splendid panorama, stopping here and there for some photos before heading to visit two monasteries: Varlaam and St. Stephens.

As contradictory as it looks, I am counting at least a dozen tourist buses lined up, surrounding each monastery. It is wonderful that we are allowed to visit them, however, once inside the monasteries, surrounded and squeezed by so many tourists, one can barely see the beautiful icons and no time to appreciate the spiritual aspect of these places, just enough to lite a candle and say a prayer amidst the cacophony of multilingual explanations of the guides.

No short pants for gentlemen and no bare shoulders or trousers for ladies inside the monasteries. At the entrance, long wraparounds are lent to the ladies; as for the men with short pants, oh well …

Monastery of St. Stephens (Agios Stefanos)

The Monastery of St. Stephens was built in the 15th Century on the site of a hermitage dating from the 12th Century. It now serves as a convent to nuns.

Monastery of Roussanou

View of the Monastery of Roussanou from the Monastery of Varlaam.

The Monastery of Roussanou was built in the 16th Century. It is now home to communities of nuns.

Holy Monastery of St. Nicholas Anapfsas (Agios Nikolaos)

The Holy Monastery of St. Nicholas Anapfsas was built on a rock of 85 meters (279 feet) high in the 14th Century but the church dates from the 16th Century.

Monastery of Varlaam (All Saints)

The Monastery of Varlaam, the second largest of the monasteries, was built in the 16th Century on the site of a hermitage dating from the 14th Century. There are 195 stairs to reach the monastery.

Monastery of Great Meteoron

- *The Monastery of Great Meteoron that sits at 400 meters (1,300 feet) high is the oldest, the largest and the highest of the monasteries. It was built in the 14th Century and expanded in the 16th Century (left).*
- *Monastery of Varlaam (right).*
- *Monastery of Roussanou (below, in the middle).*

Monastery of the Holy Trinity (Agia Triada)

The Monastery of the Holy Trinity (Agia Triada) was built in 1458-1476. Monks used ropes and baskets for transportation until 1925 where a rocky path of 140 steps was carved in the rocks.

After our tour of Meteora, on our way to the restaurant for lunch, we stop at an icon factory and store where we are served local sweet wine while contemplating the artists at work before purchasing some icons and admiring the artwork. Lunch is at a nice large and modern restaurant decorated in bright red colors. A young couple dressed in folkloric outfits greets us at the entrance. The main menu consists of meatballs and potatoes, and as usual, of great quality and tasty.

It is now 3:30 p.m. and we have a long drive ahead, about 355 km (221 miles) to Athens.

Cotton Fields in Lamia - Λαμία

Back on the road, the bus makes a stop at a cotton field for us to take some photos. Unfortunately, a ditch is separating the road from the field and we cannot cross. The farmer who spots at a distance our interest in the field arrives with his truck and distributes us some freshly picked cotton left behind in the truck. A simple gesture but so genuine and so touching. Only in Greece …

Lamia, once called Zeitouni in the Middle Ages, is situated in Central Greece, 90 km (56 miles) northeast of Delphi. 215 km (134 miles) northwest of Athens and 302 km (188 miles) south of Thessaloniki.

Late in the evening, we arrive at the same hotel in Mati by the shores of the Aegean Sea where we spent our first night in Greece. Luckily, the welcoming team of mosquitos is not around. Most probably due to the strong wind. But no matter what, I am not leaving that balcony door open tonight!

Kandylakia - Καντηλάκια

When travelling throughout Greece, the first thing one notices are these roadside shrines, built like a miniature church, called *kandylakia* placed by citizens to thank for a missed accident, for protection or in memory of a lost life. They can be made of any material: stone, wood, tin, etc. and they hold icons, holy oil, candles. Larger *kandylakias* are placed in the city as a public prayer corner.

Day 7

Athens - Αθήναι / Acropolis – Ακρόπολη

We start the day by visiting the Panathenaic Stadium in Athens. We drive by the Arch of Hadrian and through Syntagma Square, by the Parliament. We are in lively Athens!

Panathenaic Stadium – Situated in the city center, it was originally built in 330-329 BCE for Panathenaic competitions. Later, it was entirely restored with marble seats in 140-144 BCE before being abandoned until 1896 when it was excavated and restored by the benefactor George Averoff. It is now used for events and as the finishing venue for the annual Marathons. It could sit 50,000.

The Arch of Hadrian was built in 131 CE in honor of the Roman Emperor Hadrian. It is situated between Acropolis and the Temple of the Olympian Zeus (left).

George Averoff, whose monument stands at the entrance of the Panathenaic Stadium, was a Greek businessman and philanthropist who financed the restoration of the Stadium in 1895 (right).

Acropolis! The last site of our tour. Anxious to see it in person, I am already contemplating all the amazing photos that I would be taking. Alas, we are first warned by our guide to watch for our steps because through wear and tear the rocks have turned very slippery. The next challenge is not to lose the group amongst the hundreds of people going up and down the Acropolis. Added to these challenges: to follow the pace of the crowds climbing or going down the slippery steps. Stopping to take photos? Good luck!

I finally make it to the top only to be greeted by a tremendous wind and multiple groups of tourists and more tourists. I soon give up the idea of an idealistic photo of the Parthenon. Either it's surrounded by a crowd of tourists or scaffolding.

The Temple of Zeus – Its construction began in 515 BCE but only finished in 131 CE by the Roman Emperor Hadrian.

The Parthenon, built in 447-438 BCE, was formerly a temple but used primarily as a treasury. In late 6th Century, it was converted to a church and later to a mosque under the Ottoman rule. Parthenon meaning "temple of the virgin/maiden" goddess referring to Athena.

The Erechtheion is an ancient Greek Temple built in 421-406 BCE to house Athena's statue. Six Caryatids ornate the porch. The 6th Century saw it converted into a church, then into a palace by the Franks and even into a harem during the Ottoman rule in 1460.

The Theater of Dionysus was built in the 6th Century BCE at the foot of Acropolis but since it had gone several transformations. The present day excavated theater dates from 390-325 BCE.

The Odeon of Herodus was built between 160-174 CE for musical performances. Since its reconstruction in 1950, it has hosted numerous world famous artists and orchestras and remains a favorite venue.

After our last lunch with the group, at a tavern by the foot of Acropolis, consisting of chicken brochette & honey yogurt for dessert, we are on our own for two hours. Right away, I spot the hop-on, hop-off trolley in the street. The tour lasts 45 minutes. Perfect! I hop on the trolley. At least, I can say I had a glimpse of the city center, Plaka, Monastiraki and all these taverns, souvenir stores. All what makes Athens so appealing!

the grecos project
the grecos project
GREEK MEDITERANIAN FOOD

ADRIANOU str.
HELLAS
SHOPPING
PARADISE

€
5,50

The ruins of the Library of Hadrian built in 132 CE by Roman emperor Hadrian. On the left, Tzisdarakis Mosque built in the 18th Century by the Ottomans. It is now part of the Museum of Greek Folk Art.

Day 8

Last Day …

Wake up call at 5:00 a.m. The flight back is scheduled for 8:30 a.m. While waiting to board the airplane, the sun is rising on the horizon.

On the airplane, one last surprise. I am presented with a gift bag offered by the airline company: a burlap bag filled with a box of cookies, a bag of coffee and a small coffee pot. Lucky winner that I am! They really know how to entice me to return to Greece…

And while tasting those delicious cookies and writing these lines, I am reliving every moment of my short trip on a constant replay mode. This is only a prelude to my next visits …

Bibliography

Collection Encyclopédies du Voyage. *Grèce, Athènes et le Péloponnèse*. Spain: Gallimard, 2016.

Mehling, M. *Athens and Attica (Phaidon Cultural Guide)*. New York/Canada: Prentice Hall Press Travel Publishing, 1986.

Michelin et Cie. *Greece*, France: Michelin Tyre Public Limited Company, 1991.

Municipality of Nafplio. 2011. *Nafplio*. Accessed January 9, 2017. http://www.nafplio.gr/en/municipality/municipalareaofnafpliomenu/nafpliomenu.html

Municipality of Nafplio. 2011. *Tolo*. Accessed January 9, 2017. http://www.nafplio.gr/en/municipality/municipalsectionofassini/tolomenu.html

Reader's Digest Association. *Strange Worlds Amazing Places, A tour of Earth's marvels and mysteries*. London: The Reader's Digest Association Limited, 1994.

Sakoulas, Thomas. *Delphi Archeological Site. Ancient-Greece.org*. Accessed December 9, 2016. http://ancient-greece.org/history/delphi.html.

Sakoulas, Thomas. *Delphi Museum. Ancient-Greece.org*. Accessed December 9, 2016. http://ancient-greece.org/museum/muse-delphi.html

Unesco, Culture, World Heritage Centre. *Sanctuary of Asklepios at Epidaurus*. 1992-2017. Accessed January 17, 2017. http://whc.unesco.org/en/list/491.

Wikipedia contributors, "Meteora," *Wikipedia, The Free Encyclopedia*. Accessed March 2, 2017. https://en.wikipedia.org/w/index.php?title=Meteora&oldid=766105949.

About the Author

Arsinée Donoyan has been passionate about photography for more than a decade. Autodidact, she uses photography to capture the present moment and transmits it to the viewer with great sensitivity. Her photos have been exhibited in regional cultural centers where she has also participated in photography contests and been rewarded more than once. Several of her photos have been part of poetry illustrations, academic visual presentations and publications.

After a successful career as administrator and French/English translator, she now dedicates her time in projects that encompass her passion of photography, writing, history, geography, archeology and travel.

Made in United States
North Haven, CT
16 March 2022

17211175R10058